Neighborhood
Watch
You Can't Make This Stuff Up

By Heather Mottesheard

D1711900

Illustrations by Emily Mottesheard

Illustration & Cover by Emily Mottesheard

Printed in the United States of America

First Printing, 2019

ISBN 9781698870199

Mottfolio Design Publishing
149 South Oak Street
Clarksburg, WV 26301

www.mottfolio.com

Dedication

I'VE LOST COUNT of how many times Sandy and I've said that we need to write this in a book and make our first million. So, I hope this just makes you laugh enough to help me laugh all the way to the bank or the office of my investment advisor, David.

I want to thank three of my favorite female comedians for showing me how to find everything that is funny in life and people: Jeanne Robertson, Kathleen Madigan, and Chonda Pierce. I found them on Sirius Radio when we bought our first Luxury car. There are others but you were the first. Also, thanks to all the family, friends, and neighbors in my life who give me so much to be grateful for and write about. I just want to say that if you recognize yourself in this book, it is probably you because I can't make this stuff up.

Introduction

WELCOME TO MY WORLD. My friends and I live in neighborhoods called subdivisions. My neighborhood contains thirty-three lots and thirty houses. My house is the first one on the left as you enter the subdivision. My neighbor Carolyn now lives in the first house on the right. She wanted to be number one but I'm number 101. She is 102. I don't think she has ever forgiven me. It's not my fault. Homeland Security did it. Originally, the numbers were all mixed up and not in any order. As the houses were built the local postmistress just gave out numbers. My house used to be 19B. My next-door neighbor, to the left, was 21 F. When Carolyn lived in the second house on the right, across the street from me, she was 19A. The first lot didn't have a house or number yet. I'm a retired teacher/librarian, recently widowed after 43 years of marriage, with two grown children, an adorable grandson, one dog, and one cat. This is a very normal, conservative, republican, tea party, one token democrat, redneck, hillbilly, gun carrying, family neighborhood. This is my life.

You can't make this stuff up.

Chapter 1
Lawns, Groundhogs, & Religion

LAWNS ARE A BIG ISSUE in subdivisions. Each homeowner has their own approach and philosophy toward their lawn but there are certain principals that prevail. Men cut grass. When Robin decided to help her husband out because he was having a very busy week by cutting her grass, everyone became very concerned about Toby's health. Phone calls were made to check on Toby and next-door neighbors walked over to check on him. They just moved into the neighborhood from an apartment and didn't know the local customs yet. My husband Jim always cut the grass. The big twenty-four-inch, gas powered lawnmower he used was very heavy and scared me so I wouldn't use it. Toby started out with a borrowed, nineteen-inch, lawnmower then quickly purchased a twenty-four inch one. In a subdivision, manhood is measured in inches.

Jim passed away in January. One fair day in February, my neighbor came to me expressing his deep concern about the future of my lawn care with offers of any help I might need. I thought he was checking on me, but no, he was checking on my lawn care plans. The groundhog said that we were going to have an early Spring, so it was time to start preparations. I frankly had not given it much thought. I found out later that the men in my part of the neighborhood had a meeting on what should be done about my grass, with Jim gone. Jim's favorite quote of mine was; "There is no such thing as men's or women's jobs but there are certain things men just ought to do." I cut the grass once after Jim's first hip replacement. He said I cut the grass like I ran the vacuum cleaner. Three days after surgery he recut the front lawn. So, with Jim gone, I purchased a lightweight, nineteen-inch, electric lawnmower, with a cord. I think it's cute. The first time I cut the grass with it, the men were slowing down to stare as they entered the subdivision on their way home. I mow like I vacuum the carpets. I don't leave nice rows with tire marks or make checkerboard patterns, but I get it done. I think it looks more natural. I told my friend Sandy that Jim is probably looking down saying, "Shit, if I had known she would help cut the grass, I would have bought her one years ago." He probably would have still recut it.

Tom has to be the first person to cut his lawn each year. I've seen snow in shady areas while he was mowing his grass. Since the groundhog said that there was going to be an early spring, he began cutting in February. One year, Lee innocently was the first to cut his lawn and Tom was out within the hour. I made a comment about this and brought it to the attention of all the men at our end of the neighborhood. The next year four lawns were cut before Tom's. After that everyone now waits for Tom to wave the checkered flag(lawn). No one wants to inflict permanent psychological damage. Tom is a good neighbor and we like him.

It's not easy owning the adjoining lawn to Tom's. His lawn has been mowed so many times I think it is bonsai grass. In one seven-day period he cut his lawn three times. You can clearly see the property line between our properties. His grass is lower than ours. I now make sure I lower the lawnmower to the lowest setting right before I mow next to his property line so my lawn always looks lower now. Carolyn, who lives across the street, likes to look at my garden from her second story windows. She calls to congratulate me when my grass turns the same color as Tom's or is the same height. Before the summer is over, I'm going to suggest we synchronize our blade height. Harmony between neighbors must be maintained.

Everyone at our end of the neighborhood fertilizes their lawns except David. His philosophy is that the more you fertilize, the more you have to cut. He constantly tells us we are crazy every time he sees us spreading lawn care products. One year he did this so much that while he was on vacation, I bought the Scotts and Steve fertilized David's lawn. He bitterly complained about needing to cut his grass more than the usual three times in one year. Jim commiserated by remarking that the grass seemed to love the cool wet summer we were having. He never suspected. This year we are all following Tom's lead and cutting our lawns beginning in late February early March. David declared he doesn't cut till May. It's against his religion. I believe he is a Baptist.

To preserve the view from the patio they never built, David and Libby bought the lot behind them. This gave David a lot more grass to cut. Just in time he inherited an old riding lawn mower. After removing some lower limbs from their trees, Dave had a weekly grass cutting revelation. The problem is, the riding mower rarely works. He spends most Saturday mornings working on the mower instead of actually cutting any grass. I always think of the old expression; "If you can't drive it, park it and milk it". Bless his heart it's in the right place.

Leaves are a big deal in lawn care for my neighbors. I've seen Patti picking up leaves by hand. Our subdivision is called Poplar Point Estates because there were so many Poplar Trees in the area. All the Poplar Trees have been cut down because they were too messy and replaced by dogwoods. Dogwoods have little leaves that blow away quickly in the fall. Steve set the record. He had all twenty-three trees on his property cut down. He didn't want to rake leaves or mow around them. I am the only one with a Pin Oak Tree. It's leaves don't fall till December so that's OK. They blow away before grass cutting season. During the February warm spell this year, I noticed that my lawn was covered in leaves but Toms yard was bare. He was standing on his porch daring any leaves to cross the property line. I cut the front yard that day to mulch my leaves and blow them into my garden. You could see the relief on his face.

John truly has a phobia about leaves on his roof. He uses a backpack type leaf blower every day and twice a day, in the fall, on his roof. The ladder permanently leans against the roof. He never takes it down because he uses it every day to climb up on the roof to blow off the leaves. His shingles are smooth and bald. We're worried about John. His insurance replaced the roof citing wind damage.

The lawn care bible comes out every Thursday. It is the home improvement store ad in the newspaper. Every homeowner who cares scans the fliers every Thursday morning for specials on lawn equipment, plants, patio furniture, and mulch. It's like playing the stock market. When mulch is five bags for ten dollars, it's time to buy. When fertilizer went on sale at the end of the summer season, Tony and John hooked up a trailer to Tony's truck and came home with ten bags, each. February isn't that far away.

One day. Tom and I cut our grass at the same time. He finished a bit ahead of me and began spreading insect control granules on his lawn. On cue, David came out and yelled across the street to Tom that he should not use that stuff. It will make his grass grow faster. He then went back in his house. It's like watching the bird come in and out of a cuckoo clock. Tom stopped and walked over to me. "As soon as they go out of town, I'm fertilizing the front yard and your fertilizing the back!"

Chapter 2

Aliens, Weight Loss, &
Yorkshire Terriers

MY FRIEND JEAN came to visit me for a week. She lived on a dairy farm in Vermont near the Canadian border with 300 cows that her husband milked twice a day. All their milk goes to Ben and Jerry's Ice Cream. Her cows are my heroes. Jean's nearest neighbor lived miles away and she had never eaten southern fried chicken, biscuits with gravy, or knew what a hush puppy was. She dipped her French fries in brown gravy and never used ketchup. Life in a subdivision below the Mason Dixon Line was like visiting a foreign country for her. In the subdivision, in the summer, women who don't work outside the home, iron their husbands work shirt the night before, stay up late and sleep in the next morning. I told her to sleep in. Jean got up at 5:00 AM. Until she adapted, she had no choice but sit on the deck, with a bottle of water, and read a book. The timer on the coffee pot was set for nine A.M.

She was also not familiar with the responsibilities one has toward your subdivision neighbors. One reason we were sleeping late on her first morning is because we had some excitement in the middle of the night. Lynn had awakened at 2:00 AM and walked into her master bathroom. It suddenly was lit up by a very bright light coming through the second story window. This scared her and since her husband was out of town, she called us because we live across the street. She reported to my husband Jim that a spaceship had landed in her back yard and she wanted him to investigate. Jim didn't say a word. He pulled on a pair of jeans and walked across the street. The people who had owned the house before Lynn had a street light installed on a telephone pole that lite up the back yard. The timer had gotten thrown off and decided to wait till 2:00 AM to come on. After reassuring Lynn we went back to bed. At 4:00AM the phone rang. Lynn's garage was flooding. Jim pulled his jeans back on, walked barefoot to her garage and turned off the water valve her garden hose was attached to. The hose had split.

At 9:20 AM Jean and I were drinking coffee when the doorbell rang. In walks Lynn. She was wearing bright blue eye shadow, a full length bright pink fuzzy robe, and matching fuzzy slippers with her long flowing bleached blond hair hanging down her back. She needed to weigh herself and she knew I had three different scales. (Don't ask why. It's a long story.) Her own scale showed she had gained three pounds and that was impossible. It must be broken so she threw it away. We sat my three in a row, in the hallway. Lynn unzipped her robe and kicked off the slippers. She was now wearing a wife beater, men's t-shirt, men's boxer shorts, and no underwear or bra. After trying each scale, she picked the one that she weighed the least on, zipped back into the robe, put on slippers, thanked me for the scale, and walked out the door with it. I now only have two scales.

At ten forty-five the doorbell rang. It was Kelly. Her eyes were outlined in black. She had waist length jet black hair. She was wearing a black satin negligee, a flowing leopard print voile bathrobe, high-heeled, clear plastic bedroom slippers with purple pompoms on the toes, and carrying a Yorkshire Terrier dog. As she click-clacked down the hall, she apologized for interrupting, but she was out of coffee and if her mother-in- law woke up and didn't get coffee the day would be ruined. I provided the coffee, she click-clacked back down the hall calling out her thanks. As I sat back down on the deck with Jean, she looked at me and asked, "Do you have any other neighbors?"

Oh, yes, I do!

Chapter 3

One Sexy Fireman, Good Luck Shovels, Guns, & Revolution

IN THIS NEIGHBORHOOD, we all built our own homes and raised our children within feet of each other. We've bonded. You lend a hand and help your neighbor if you can. We know all about each other. We keep each other under surveillance watching for any signs of change or problems but otherwise we mind our own business.

When Howard was away during the first gulf war, his grass was cut each week and his garbage cans were pulled out and in. After Jim died, Lee pulls my garbage can out Thursday morning and rolls it back. When the outside lights burnt out, Toby brought over his ladder and changed them. Food appeared, sidewalks had snow removed, and driveways were cleared. Libby makes sure my door is locked and she has even closed the garage door while I ran errands.

When Bob was driving into the neighborhood he saw a man struggling to load his horses onto a trailer. He stopped and helped the man load the horses. He didn't know the horses were stolen from a nearby farm. Paul made horse sounds every time he saw Bob for weeks. No good deed goes unpunished.

On hot summer days, teenagers often come to a bridge near the entrance to the subdivision to jump into the river and swim. It's a free way to cool off. Bless his heart, a new neighbor called 911 when he saw a boy jumping off the bridge because he thought the young man was committing suicide. Bless the Sheriff's Department. I'm sure as teenagers they cooled off that way a few times. They kept straight faces and didn't laugh once at the scene. Very professional.

When we were building our house, Jim was rushing to get the water line connected to the house. He was standing waist deep in the ditch hurrying because a storm was due within the hour. As the neighbors were coming home after work, they stopped, parked their trucks, and jumped in to help. The water line was connected, and the ditch filled before the storm hit and the men got home in time for supper. One of our shovels got buried in the ditch but we felt like that was for good luck.

When the house across from Tom had a fire, Tom didn't hesitate when Dena ran to his house for help. Tom made sure everyone was out of the house and called the Fire Department. He cleared the garage removing the cars and riding mower. Tom lounges at home in a pair of white 70's era gym shorts and no shirt. The whole time he was working with neighbors and Firemen to make sure everyone and the property was safe, he was wearing his favorite gym shorts. In the dark they looked like underwear. Tom was voted the sexiest Fireman in the neighborhood.

It was February, about 20 degrees and a stranger was spotted roaming behind houses at the other end of the subdivision. Tom and Jim were called because we are the last houses on our end. Walt and Jr. were on their way down the street, joining neighbors on the way, all bearing arms. Tom was in his gym shorts with gun and holster. Jim said, "I'm coming out, just don't shoot me." He was the only one who didn't have a gun. The stranger was pinned down by Tom's wood pile. He swam across the river to get away and hasn't come back. The men figured that a cold swim was enough of a deterrent against any future desire to snoop through the neighborhood. There were enough guns in this neighborhood for a small revolution. It gives you a comforting feeling.

Chapter 4

Holiday Traditions, Blow-ups, & Vegetables On The Porch

EVERYONE in a southern subdivision decorate for the holidays and different seasons in some way. We tend to do this with abundance. There are wreaths on the doors and garden flags flying. There are also large flags on poles declaring support for sports teams. The decorations start taking on a life of their own in the fall of the year moving into a big finish with Christmas. An exchange student from Thailand asked my son why people put vegetables on their porches in September. Try to explain Jack-o-lanterns, hay bales, scarecrows, and corn stalks to that young man.

With Christmas comes lights. That is fun and pretty, but every neighborhood has a National Lampoon House. I like the lights and appreciate the efforts to sync them up to music, if that's your thing. I have a wreath for every possible category plus a coordinating garden flag and mailbox cover. Our Lampoon House also decorates with blow-up decorations. They have every one ever made lined up on their lawn in straight rows. It looks like the Macy's parade on crack. I just want to take a large needle and….. These people have a garage sized building just to store their collection. WOW! Where is the art in that? They are nice people, so we just drive by and wave.

If you live in one place long enough, traditions develop. In 1978, family friends gave us a bag of used Christmas lights. They were the old large glass multi colored bulbs that burn out every five minutes and break if you look at them in the wrong way. I drooped them from the railing of our deck. This was simple and festive. I was afraid to use them inside for fear they would burn down the house. The lights can be seen from across the river and up and down the river road. Houses on the hills surrounding our house can see them. I didn't realize at the time, but I had started a tradition.

Replacement bulbs were costing a fortune and the light sets were falling apart. It is almost impossible to find yellow bulbs. Ten years into this tradition, I made a change. I drooped clear twinkle lights from the deck railing to match the front porch. Pre-lit garland from Walmart is cheap, safe, and easy. If it stops working, just throw it away and buy another. I started to get calls. Apparently, as people were coming home at night during that time of the year, the colored lights cheered them up. It's dark by five o'clock and they looked forward to seeing the lights. I had no idea this was happening. Perfect strangers called neighbors to ask about why the change had been made. They stopped me in the grocery store to express concern. The lights were discussed during church fellowships. I changed the lights. I now use modern, traditional look, multi-color, plastic, LED, size "C", Christmas lights. If you are responsible for a tradition within a neighborhood community, you better take it seriously. I put it in my will along with the deed to the house.

Chapter 5
Mailboxes, Rob Reiner, & Culture

MAILBOXES ARE A BIG DEAL in the neighborhood. Some of us take them more seriously than others. They are a part of the American culture. I'm referring to the kind that sits out near the street or road in front of your house or property on some kind of a post. They are their own art form. Artists feature them in paintings, Jeff Foxworthy talks about his "male" box, they have been main characters in movies, and TV Shows. I recognize the sound of the motor our mail person's car makes as she drives through the neighborhood. That's how the dog and I know when the mail is here. He always barks. Companies have formed to manufacture mailboxes to satisfy every taste. Folk artist's creations are unlimited.

In our subdivision there are many individual approaches to this icon. I have mine surrounded by a flower garden, four flower pots are mounted on the post, and there is a decorative cover over the box. Others are enclosed in brick posts, or just have numbers on the side of a plastic box. They have no imagination. The post office has many regulations that deal with mailboxes, but we just smile and nod. Who is going to put a stamp in a loaf of pumpkin bread placed in a mailbox because someone wasn't home when it was delivered. My recipe makes three loaves. I have to share.

I've had at least seven different boxes and posts. Depending on the materials used, mailboxes occasionally need to be replaced. I started with a simple wooden post but now have a very classy white molded plastic colonial post and box assembly. I came to the realization that every time the movie "Stand by Me" is shown on TV, my mailbox got destroyed. There is a scene showing the boys driving by hitting mailboxes with a baseball bat. Rob Reiner, you owe me for four mailboxes. The present one has a core, made out of steel, and anchored on a transmission line pipe. (The oil and gas industry will know what I'm talking about.) The last kid that hit that box with a baseball bat broke his arm. Don't mess with my box.

It's art!

Chapter 6

Helicopters, Waiting For The Other Shoe To Drop, & An Old Coot

OLD COOT LIVED in an old trailer across the river from my house on land owned by his family. The trailer was old and built long before any safety standards existed. I never learned his real name. He had chickens running around the property, that Brent had given him, until he ate them all. He traded horses to supplement his Social Security income. On mild summer nights he sat on the trailer steps and drank beer. Not long after we built the house, we were sleeping with the windows open. I love doing that before you have to close up the house and turn on the air conditioner. Jim didn't. He would just sleep and sweat. About two in the morning, Old Coot broke out into song. Our Basset Hound, Big Mac, rested his mouth on the window seal and joined in. Aawahoo! Aawaahooooo! Big Mac was very talented. Old Coot decided to join the chorus. Aawahoo! Aawaahooooo! The neighbors referred to this as "night song". One summer, while Old Coot was away, something exploded inside the trailer and it burnt to the ground in ten minutes. The top and bottom of that trailer was flat on the ground. Old Coot didn't return, and the mild summer nights have never been the same.

There are other sounds in the night. There is a stop sign at the end of Doc Bailey Road across the river from our house. If you don't stop, you cross the river road and roll down the bank into the river. You can turn right, left, or swim. All night long tires screech as drivers slow to make the turn. It was like living near the railroad tracks, after time you just don't notice it anymore. One night the screeching tires ended with a car plunging down the river bank. It was like hearing the other shoe finally drop and it woke me up. I started shaking Jim awake. "It happened! It finally happened!" One time, as the driver crawled out, the car exploded. What a spectacular sight. I've had to report so many wrecks that the Sheriff's Department recognizes my voice. We put up a sign on the river bank, shaped like a stop sign that says, "OOPS". It's the last thing drivers see as they plunge off the road.

The bridge near my house is used for many things besides crossing the river and a diving board for a summer swims. During the night you hear splashing as people drop trash off the bridge into the river. One night the splashing was particularly loud numerous. State Police divers found all the safes stolen from local businesses below the bridge. Another time, thieves through stolen guns off the bridge. The only problem was; the river was frozen. All the guns and rifles just laid on the ice for the State Police to walk out and pick up. One of the more serious uses for the bridge was as a place to land emergency helicopters. This is fine but as they arrive, they pass over my house, blowing leaves into my deck. I mentioned this to the pilot during a Boy Scout Safety Fair. He had no idea. Could he not fly back over and blow the leaves off the deck? Since then the State Police buzz my house every chance they get. Sometimes they do this in the middle of the night. It keeps the deck clean. These are wonderful public servants.

Chapter 7
Family Funerals, Southern Belles, & Bingo

LIVING IN A SUBDIVISION, you could find yourself going to at least one funeral a week. There are very few steps of separation between family and neighbor's cousin twice removed. I don't go to funerals unless I really have to. They are getting to Egyptian-ish for me. They cost a lot of money and are hard on the family. I've observed that they tend to attract people you don't really want to associate with. Because of his job position, Jim was obligated to go to many funerals. This was something that was very difficult and sad. My husband and I were private people. We didn't want attention and we didn't seek it. Jim told me if I spend a lot of money on a funeral, he would haunt me. He said this after a friend's sister spent $20.000.00 on an extra-large coffin for her abusive husband who weighed over 800 pounds when he died. By the time she finished the arrangements, the funeral was close to fifty thousand dollars. Jim couldn't understand putting that much money into the ground. Cremation would have been less than a tenth of that. Jim didn't get a funeral. His ashes are in a pirate chest, on a book case. I don't want to be haunted. I watch "Dead Files" on Saturday night and believe it's real.

I went to my husband's cousin William's funeral. Jim had to take his mother and he told me he couldn't do this alone. Jim's mother doesn't have any filters or know how to whisper. As soon as we arrived at the Funeral Home Becky walked straight up to the casket and looked in. "Is that really William? I haven't seen him in years." She demanded of his daughter Anne. Anne said, "Don't you think he looks so good?" Becky announced, "How good can he look? He's ninety-eight years old and he is dead!" Jim took his mother's arm and suggested we get a seat. Two rows up, Anne's daughter and her husband were "making out". Jim's cousin Margie strolled in wearing a white, full skirted, shirt waist dress, with four-inch, horizontal, black stripes along the full length of the dress. The dress made me think of bumble bees. After making her entrance she chose to sit on the loveseat in front of us. This allowed her enough space for her to spread out her skirt. Once settled she turned and looked at Becky. "Oh Becky, sooo good to see yooou! You look sooo gooood!" Jim leaned forward and remarked that she cleaned up well. I was next in line. "Oh, Heather darling, it is so wonderful to see you, you precious darling girl!" Margie fancies herself a high society southern belle with influence. I just smiled. Jim got told how handsome he was and what a good son he was to come with his mama. Anne's daughter and her husband really needed to get a room at this point.

Right before the service started Becky asked, in a voice the whole assembly could hear, "Isn't it time for this thing to get started?" Right before the first hymn, "Amazing Grace", was played, Becky asked, "Aren't they going to play "Amazing Grace?" Right before they recited the Lord's Prayer, Becky asked, "Aren't they going to say the Lord's Prayer?" Right before the minister read the service, Becky asked, "Aren't they going to have a minister read a service?" Right before the last hymn was played, Becky said, "This thing should be over soon. If William had any friends, they would be dead by now." Jim rose and walked his mother to the exit. It had started to rain. The funeral director was passing out umbrellas and asking if we were going to the graveside. Becky didn't want, "a cheap umbrella that leaked" and told him, "Hell no. I'm not going to get pneumonia for him." I stayed with Becky while Jim got the car. We took Becky to eat because, "Funerals make me hungry and the family was too cheap to serve food." I enjoyed that funeral. I was a precious darling girl with a handsome husband who is good to his mama.

When Jim's cousin Charles died not to long after William's funeral, I told Jim I wouldn't miss this for the world. I called and told Becky when we would be picking her up. Margie, the southern belle, was Charles's wife. She provided a big write-up for him in both the morning and evening papers plus the Sunday edition. I didn't know that people sent invitations to funerals. Margie did. The First Presbyterian Church Chapel was full. The funeral was really just a memorial service because Margie donated Charles's body to the University. If we had known this ahead of time we might have been able to prepare Jim's mother for the experience. As soon as we were seated the questions began. "Where's the coffin?" "How can you have a funeral without a coffin?" "What University?" "What does the University want his body for?" The funeral service continued to the mausoleum. "Why did she buy one of these slots if there was no coffin?" "It's five across and five down, just like a bingo card. It will be easy to remember which square he isn't in." Jim's mother does not disappoint.

Cousin Carolyn died in her late thirties after a long struggle with cancer. Her boys were in grade school at the time and it was all very sad for the family. Carolyn's family were members of the Catholic Church. They had a full Catholic service that included a procession of the casket down the aisle with the family walking behind. At the end of the service, the family and casket procession went back up the aisle.

Becky, "They're having another G... d... parade."

That was Becky's last funeral.

Chapter 8

Who Are Your People? Basset Hounds, & Moonshine

WHEN YOU FIRST MOVE into a southern neighborhood or get married, you must answer a lot of questions because a connection has to be made. You used to work with somebody's cousin. Your related by marriage to a former neighbor. You belong to the same political party. Once the connection is established, your accepted and your told everyone's life story. You need to be ready to name your family members back several generations. My husband's family was a problem. It took me time to sort them out because some of them had two sets of names. Jack was called John, Hugh was Pops, Annetta was Biscuit, Charles was Tubby, Joyce was Becky, Margaret was Margie, and Violet was Rose. Jim's grandfather was Ale and his brother was Oat. They made moonshine for a living. A neighbor's grandfather remembered buying the beverage from them. A connection was made and I was accepted. When Jim and I became engaged, his cousin came to me and said he had two questions: "Are you a Republican?" and "Can you spell it?" Since I was and I could, I was in!

Julie is a real, good friend. Actually, we are family. We became family because of our dogs and mutual friends. Barbara decided that my family would be the perfect home for Big Mac, a Basset Hound Virginia had. Virginia breed and showed champion Basset Hounds. Big Mac needed a family and Barbara decided we needed a Basset Hound. The day after Christmas we piled into the car and picked Mac up. Thus, begins the connection. Over the year,s Julie and I adopted Virginia's dogs and became good friends. She had Rocky, Pebbles, Tiffany, Wendy, and Carly. I had Mac, Max, Tad, and now Hambone. Virginia left Hambone to me in her will. Julie got Carly and Wendy. All the dogs are from the same family blood line. You can't be more connected than that.

Sandy and I are sure we are related. Jim's Aunt Ruth's first marriage was to his cousin Bill. She really isn't an aunt, but she wanted to be called that since she was so much older than us. Ruth was from a small town near the neighborhood I live in and has family in the town Sandy is from so we must be related in some way. We have been through many things together, from Homeroom Mothers, PTO, deaths, stalkers, births, concession stands, marriages, to vacations. We have bonded. I'm sure we are related under the southern rules of connection.

I recently helped Sandy with a dinner at her church. Our philosophy is: Feed the body and you feed the soul. Sarah came to help because she is aunt Ruth's niece and she wanted to see me. It had been several years, so we had a lot of catching up to do. Before the night was over I knew who had died and what they died from, who had married and divorced, where everyone had gone on vacation, what medical conditions they were being tested for, how many children were born, and were they all lived. A minimum of three hugs and it's time to go home. Kissing cousins are family too. Instead of six degrees of separation, there is only one, in my world.

Chapter 9

Neighborhood Organization, The Mafia, & Caller ID

EVERYONE KNOWS EVERYONE in the neighborhood. Southern Neighborhoods have organization. There is usually one or two women who spearhead this task. They take care of the annual picnic, yard sale, Lining the street at Christmas with luminaries, and update the list of neighbors with addresses and phone numbers. Southern ladies like to have their social lives organized and themed. All social and holiday customs need to be observed.

Our neighborhood also has a girl mafia. This group of women have husbands who are doctors with long hours at the hospital. They are connected via cell phone and depend on each other for life, liberty, and the pursuit of happiness. They don't do anything without each other or make a decision without a thorough satellite enabled discussion. Their main job is to hold parties. Everything from Tupperware to sexy underwear has an in-home party. The problem is, once one person has a party, every member of the mafia has to have one too. That's seven each. They cluster together in church vestibules and school hallways. They don't do anything without each other. The rest of us are mere filler for the guest list. If you are going to safely and pleasantly live in the same neighborhood with these women, you better have a line item section of your budget for their home parties. My husband provided me with a pie chart showing it in our household budget.

Heaven forbid that one of these ladies has a crisis and can't get in touch with the mafia. Summer vacation time is peak season for these crisis. My phone rang when Linda ate spicy food during her third pregnancy and got indigestion. She needed someone to tell her it was OK to chew some Tums. Her cat spits up a fur ball, her 4 year old, terror of a son, was hiding somewhere in the house, she felt like drinking peppermint tea and needed someone to go to the store, the cat was meowing differently, which Longaberger hostess basket should she get, etc. I was the first person to get caller ID.

Soon the rest of the "filler" group did too. You have to be creative to survive because you don't want to hurt anyone's feelings. My husband said if he wanted a woman that couldn't handle things or make decisions during the day, he wouldn't have married one with a library card. I'm a librarian. I guess that and a good credit rating made me a good catch, in his opinion, and got me through the day.

Chapter 10

Grocery Shopping, The American Flag, & Tinnitus

WHEN YOU FIRST START SHOPPING for yourself, it is exciting. You have a real sense of freedom and you can get whatever you want. It teaches you money management, budget, and the cost of nutrition. Merilee found macaroni and cheese dinners ten for $5.00. This diet lead to a very bad case of constipation.

When you have small children, this trip to the grocery store, without the children, can be the highlight of your week. You actually look forward to the only time you are going to have to yourself. If my daughter was with me, she never stopped talking and picked out the next serial killer to say hi too. Her voice became the white noise that shut down my brain function. My son would read every sign and label. I'll never forgive the teacher who taught him how to read. My husband calculated cost per ounce on everything I put in the cart. I love them, but I'd rather go alone. God bless them.

You used to have one grocery store to go to. Now I have a variety, from traditional and discount to large variety stores. Everyone sells milk, ice, and mulch. I know which one is going to be too cold so I take a sweater. I know which store handles coupons the best, and where to grab a bag of ice on the way home because you forgot it at the first store. Shopping has become more of an art form. In my area, you don't want to go to Walmart on Tuesday or Thursday mornings because that is when the senior citizens are bused to the store. They clog up the isles, fight over riding carts, run you down with riding carts, ask you to reach stuff, and get lost. I saw one lady get a wheel stuck under a display shelf and it took two employees to free her. The Walmart store had to ask the Senior Groups to spread out the number of people they transport to the store at one time because they didn't have enough of the riding carts and fights were breaking out. They needed extra staff on hand to help everyone have a successful shopping experience and make it out the correct door for the van. The best time for Walmart is Wednesday evenings while everyone is in church. It pays to be a sinner. Bless their hearts.

Grocery shopping can be entertaining. If you go to my local Walmart on Sunday afternoon about 2:00 you will see Patrick. There are some very funny videos on line about people you see at Walmart but my neighborhood has its own celebrity different from the everyday variety of Jeff Foxworthy fashion dos and don'ts for the Redneck. Patrick is a local lawyer, husband and father. He is a nice person and a good citizen. He is also a cross dresser on Sunday afternoons at the local Walmart. I first saw Patrick in court while I was serving on Jury Duty. He wore a brown tweed business suite, carried a brown leather briefcase, with a brown purse over his shoulder and had his finger nails painted red. His most memorable outfit is his patriotic ensemble that he debuted July 4th 2000. I needed onions for the hot dogs and he parked beside me that day. Picture a tall thin man with white tights, red sequined high heels, blue sequined mini skirt, red sequined crop top with a large white star on the front, American flag earrings, bare midriff, with a red sequined top hat. He threatened to sue the store if the employees didn't stop staring at him. Bless his heart, he was just being patriotic.

My sister in law decided that her mother had reached the point that she needed some help doing her grocery shopping. Ten minutes in the store, my husband got a call from his sister. Her mother had stressed her out so much that her blood pressure rose and triggered an attack of her tinnitus. She needed Jim to come and "take over" helping their mother. Jim found his sister lying on a bench in front of the store with a trash can nearby in case she threw up. He called his nephew to come help Pam get home then went to find his mother somewhere in the store. He found her. A little five foot nothing lady with gray pin curls using the shopping cart as a walker with her cane hanging on the handle. "It's about time somebody got here. I can't reach around that fat lady to get the barbecue sauce." Bless her heart. She has no filters.

Chapter 11

Smart Cars, The Olympic Flag, & Flower Boxes

W HEN I HEARD THAT THERE is more technology in our cars than was in Apollo 13, it all came home to me. I got the movie out and watched it again. They only had two floppy discs to get to the moon and back. It took the same to boot up my first computer. I just made an appointment to get my state car inspection. Robert asked if the car needed anything else and I said that the car had not mentioned anything else. I'm sure if it did, it would tell me. The car has a better computer than my brain.

The first luxury car my husband and I bought was a revelation. It had been ten years since the last time we bought a car and at the time, I was excited that it had power windows. The salesman tried to show us all the bells and whistles on the new car. We were overwhelmed but nodded like we understood. As we took off down the interstate, we couldn't find the lights. We did find that we could put it on automatic and let it run itself. Thank goodness for that because we had suddenly joined the Clampett family and felt like we were in an episode of the Beverly Hillbillies. "What's that bell?" Oh, put your seat belt on, close the door, put the car in park, close the back hatch, put the key back in the car, make a right turn in 200 feet, buy gas, put air in the tires, change the oil, make a U turn, have you enjoyed your free Sirius Radio, and watch where you going. My husband said, "Oh great. Now I have another woman in my life telling me what to do."

The symbol for this first luxury car always reminds me of the Olympic symbol. Now I call them the four rings of hell. It has ten computers placed throughout the car. The battery is located under the driver seat. If the battery goes bad or is replaced, the security system will not allow the car to be "jumped". It has to be towed and the computers reset at a dealership. In all, it costs $500.00 dollars to replace a battery. This car needed six in ten years. I suggested that there was a problem causing this and was told that I was keeping the key too close to the car. When we bought a new car, I asked where the battery was. The salesman said he had never been asked that before. I told him that it was a deal breaker. This turned out to be the tip of the ice burg for that money pit. I'm not going to talk about the lack of competent service we got from the dealership or the amount of money this car has cost us over the years because it isn't funny. Right now, the son in law of a neighbor, has it once again sitting at the dealership who are trying to get it to talk to the diagnostic computer, so they can reset another battery and find out what else is not working. It apparently doesn't want to communicate. Ron is a godsend. He still wants the car and is researching a way to get it to run again. If this car does not run I'm going to paint it pink, put it in the front yard with flower boxes under the windows. The perfect lawn ornaments. Bless it's heart, it took 42 hours to find that the main computer needed to be replaced. It now has nine more to go.

Every man in the neighborhood has become involved in the continuing saga of the car. I text daily progress reports to friends. Soon you will be able to follow its progress on line once we finish setting up the web site. The ending to this story is after 42 hours and two new computers, the dealership finally got the car communicating. Ron drove it home, spent another $5,000.00, took it in for one recall, went on vacation, came home, and it wouldn't start.

Meantime either buy an American Luxury car

without a security system from Area 51, or trade your foreign Luxury car every two years right before the warranty expires. We got our Lincoln in Kentucky and had it programed to understand a Southern Hillbilly. It lets me know if it needs anything and the battery is under the hood, in plain sight, where it belongs. Now, I take my car to a maintenance department of my choice and they talk to the car to see what it needs. We can all understand each other.

Chapter 12
Senior Citizens, Alice In Wonderland, Zombies, & Floods

WRITING THIS BOOK of stories is on my bucket list of retirement activities. I looked forward to finally have the time to do things that had to be put off because of other responsibilities. I made a list of all the women who achieved greatness during the second half of their lives. I wasn't aspiring to greatness, just a short bucket list that included painting, playing the piano, gardening, reading, writing, and travel. Little did I know what would be involved in becoming a Senior Citizen. I thought I would be continuing on in the same but more simple and peaceful life path. Well, dream on Alice.

Starting with retirement wasn't too bad. As a teacher and librarian, I was used to forms. No problem, there. When asked how I was adjusting to retirement, I said it took me seconds. I put the iron and ironing board in the closet and started staying up late and sleeping in. I had to train the dog to do the same but he adjusted. Then my husband became ill and passed away suddenly. Life changing events come all at once. Talk about forms, I'm on a new learning curve and file folder number 47. On top of learning about estates, investments, medical bills, and every day business, I turned sixty-five. Nothing prepared me for the amount of mail and phone calls you receive starting six months before you turn sixty-five. This is also a national election year which means ten to twenty survey and toll free calls a day. I was never so important in my life. I didn't know that I needed a stair climber, end of life insurance, a condo in Florida, a walk-in tub and an opinion on presidential candidates. I upgraded my phones to be able to block a hundred numbers and wore out two paper shredders. Take that scammer. I have enough shredded paper for the next presidential parade. Maybe the next president will want a ticker tape parade in New York City. Since they don't use ticker tape, he can have my paper.

At this new phase of our lives, some of us have older parents to deal with. Both Jim's and my parents have passed away, so our work has been done. I can now sit back, sympathize with friends, enjoy their stories and experiences, and write it down. Deanna's mother has always been a character. A group of ladies were going on a day long shopping trip. It involved a three-hour bus trip to the shopping destination. Deanna's mother settled into her seat, changed her shoes to travel slippers, inflated a neck pillow, positioned a lap robe and opened a bag of cheese naps and mints. We all marveled at her survival skills during our midway break at a rest stop. She slept through the break.

Parts of our area experienced some devastating flooding. Deanna went to her mother's home and tried to get her to leave and spend the night with her, just in case the flooding became as serious as predicted. At the least, her mother's home could be cut off or be without electricity. She refused to see the need. She would ride it out. Deanna' sister went to stay with her mother because she seemed to have more influence and they didn't want her stranded alone. At four in the morning the National Guard came to inform them of the mandatory evacuation. Deanna's mother said to not open the door. It was a conspiracy and ISIS had been trying to recruit her. When her daughter opened the basement door, water was up to the last three steps.

Deanna's mom said, "You need to go down and unplug the iron." Sister, "Mom, let's go. The water is up to the driveway and we have to get the car out." Mom, "I need to pack the good toothpaste, not the cheap stuff you made me buy." Sister, "Get in the Car!" Deanna's sister dropped their mother off at her house at five that morning and went back to her own home. Tag you're it. During the next night Mrs. Taylor had to be coaxed back into the house after it had been cleared of a zombie invasion. Since then Deanna's mother has settled into a beautiful assisted living community. She is now safe from zombies and ISIS recruiters. Is this me in the future? Bless my daughter's heart. Paybacks can be hell.

Chapter 13
Dead Birds, Laundry Shoots, Walt Disney, Medical Science, & The Presbyterian Church

WHEN I WAS GROWING UP, if there were five children in your family, you were a Catholic Family. There were five children in the Jones Family, but they were Presbyterians. For some reason, they didn't realize that they were supposed to only have 2.3 children. I was close to Kathy and Mark. We went to the same church, lived in the same neighborhood, went to the same schools, close in age, and spent a lot of time playing together as children. Their house was a fantastic place to be as a child. Mrs. Jones didn't get upset about anything, much. Supervision was minimal. The philosophy for child development was that if you were smart enough, you would learn. A Siamese cat lived on top of the refrigerator that swiped at people as they walked by. A Basenji dog roamed the house bumping into furniture, forgetting to duck under tables, and barking only at family members. Basenji are supposed to bark but Steve taught him how.

Our favorite thing to do was to put things down the laundry shoot. It was the only house in the neighborhood with one. Because of the number of people living in the house, laundry was a big deal. Mrs. Jones had a large wooden bin situated below the laundry shoot in the basement. It was six-foot square, four feet deep and on wheels. To smart, imaginative children, this presented many fun possibilities. There was always dirty laundry in the bin. Basically, this meant that anything dropped down the shoot would have a soft landing. At first, we tested with dolls and stuffed animals. Kathy's screams echoed on par with the best B movie thrillers when she slid down the shoot. The absolute best sounds came from the cat and then Mrs. Jones when the cat jumped out of the bin at her when she went to add a load into the washer.

Our next favorite thing to do as imaginative smart

children left on their own was to reenact Disney movies. Since there was a big tree in the front yard that had never been trimmed it was great for climbing. There were three Disney movies involving trees. I was Pollyanna climbing out the bedroom window, Hayley Mills again "In Search of the Castaways", and Dorothy McGuire in "Swiss Family Robinson". Mark played all the animals because he was going to be a doctor when he grew up. Don't ask. He was also the doctor if someone got hurt because he had a real stethoscope.

I can still see Mark standing in the basement window, telling us to watch his new trick, as he urinated through the diaphragm of the stethoscope and the urine came out the ear pieces shooting out in opposite directions after crossing in the middle. He also collected dead animals we found in the yard or neighborhood. There were mainly birds, but the collection also included chipmunks, mice, moles and one small disgusting groundhog. Mark wanted to eventually dissect them.

To preserve the animals, we placed them in the freezer located in the basement. Mrs. Jones stored extra meat in it that she found on special. It was towards the end of the summer when Mrs. Jones opened the freezer to get hamburger and discovered our collection of dead animals. You could hear her screaming for Mark five houses away. I can still see Mark running out of the house and diving under the forsythia bush to hide. He got a dissecting kit for Christmas and later did become a doctor. It truly was the most fun house in the neighborhood.

Chapter 14

Bathrooms, Loud Spice & "Hava Nagila"

WEST VIRGINIA is almost Heaven to us. Our neighborhoods are safe pleasant places. You may be living in another part of the country, but West Virginia is always your home state. When asked where you are from it is always West Virginia but you are presently living …. We do like to travel and see the rest of the country and the world. No matter where we go, we don't change. It's a small state in a small world and we can spot each other.

One of the prime places West Virginians go is Myrtle Beach. We refer to it as the West Virginia

Riviera, Mecca, or the Holy Land. It doesn't matter whether you are in a campground, cottage, condo, or hotel nearly every West Virginian knows exactly where that is.

One year, when my children were in High School, the word went out among the teenagers that if you were going to be at Myrtle Beach the last week in June, meet at Planet Hollywood at 2:30 on Wednesday. Sixty-three people showed up from a town with a population of one-thousand. We took over the restaurant. It was OK because most of the wait staff was from West Virginia too. We went from table to table taking pictures and talking. Even though we all had indoor plumbing, we were fascinated by the bathrooms. We took pictures of our reflections in the mirror that was shaped like a pair of sunglasses and sampled all the perfumes in the women's bathroom. Everyone then moved to the men's bathroom to take pictures with the mirror shaped like a shark. We all bought t-shirts and stole Planet Hollywood swizzle sticks. We took eight extra friends of our teens, to our cottage, for the night. Five of the girls stopped along the way to get their belly buttons pierced. It's a beach tradition to alter your appearance in some way. We labeled them "Fat Spice, Wet Spice, Loud Spice, Sweet Spice, and Spacey Spice.

Sometimes we travel in family groups. At the time three families shared a cottage we formed a caravan and stayed connected via C B radios since this was before

57

cell phones. Of course, everyone had to have a handle. Two of the women who happened to be widows driving black cars, were the "Black Widows". Merrilee, who made it the longest trip to the beach on record because of all her bathroom stops, was labeled "Wizzer". We had truck drivers all along the east coast complaining about us to the FCC.

West Virginia has beautiful parks and campgrounds. It takes a week to plan and pack for a family camping trip and a week to unpack. We have a lovely home, on a river that is surrounded by trees and mountains with no cell service. Why do we pack the whole house and move to a park, to camp on a river surrounded by trees and mountains, for a week? Someone mentioned a change of scenery and no cell service. The scenery was the same and we have no cell service! It took me years to finally have this epiphany. Picture a van packed tight with equipment, seven people and two Basset Hounds seated inside with a large car top carrier duct taped on the roof. An eighteen-foot pop up camper was being towed with a canoe and four bicycles mounted on top of it. There were friends following in their pickup truck with firewood piled in the back for evening campfires. Their dog was on top of the wood pooping. Friends stopped and waved as we drove through town.

In the early 60's, my parents bought a new car and my mother decided that she wanted to tour New England to see the colorful leaves in the Fall. I spent two weeks in the back seat of a car, with my hypochondriac sister, without air-conditioning while my parents pointed out the trees and deer along the roads. Three days into this odyssey I realized that New England looked very much like West Virginia. West Virginia is in the heart of the Appalachian Mountains which extend up through the state of Maine. We have the same trees and deer in our yard. I did my best to sleep through the trip and kept my mouth shut.

What fascinated me about the Caribbean was seeing my houseplants growing wild everywhere and hearing every steel drum band play "Country Roads". It's the unofficial State Song of West Virginia. The problem was that these bands always played it to a calypso beat. We were with a group of tourists in Jamaica when the band began the Caribbean version of "Country Roads". You can only take so much. Simultaneously my husband walked over and picked up a guitar. Another man picked up the other guitar and the third picked the banjo. As they began to perform the song correctly twelve more people stepped forward to sing. We were all from West Virginia. The band members were thrilled with an authentic performance by native West Virginians. Thank you, thank you very much! Apparently, there are Americans and then there are West Virginian Americans.

On a cruise to Alaska, we found ourselves on the Canadian border at the Yokan River. We were to be amazed at being at an elevation of 3,703 feet. Spruce Knob West Virginia is at 4,862 feet. The guide pointed out the granite rocks, windblown pine trees, and enthusiastically promised we would see a waterfall on our way down the mountain. The area looked much like Spruce Knob. West Virginia has 275 waterfalls above ground and higher one's underground. She was so excited about this, we figured she must have been from the Midwest. We learned that the raven is sacred in the Inuit culture. My brother in law said, "Don't we call them crows?" We stopped to look at a collection of totem poles featuring the work of a famous totem carver. Bob, from West Virginia, mentioned that he had a neighbor who carved bears in tree trunks with a chainsaw. Our most exciting time was talking to our daughter, five time zones away, across a continent using our new cell phones. We finally had cell service. Now that's amazing.

We got a chance to go to New York City. This was a hillbilly tour of the big city. We saw the main sites, three Broadway Plays, and shopped at Tiffany's. Sterling Silver is on third floor along with the most amazing bathrooms. They are all marble with twelve-foot ceilings, oversized wooden doors, and gold fixtures. Now that is class. I regret I didn't have my camera. We took our shoes off in central Park and cooled them in the water park which is a very small, long, concrete trough. We saw the carousel and the girls posed in front of limousines at Tavern on the Green. Our son participated in a charity concert at Carnegie Hall with the Barbershop Harmony Society, so now he can say he sang at Carnegie Hall. I learned how to pronounce Swarovski and saw myself on the big screen at Times Square. The whole city was celebrating cultural diversity. Sandy came face to face with a large snake wrapped around a man's body along the Puerto Rican pride parade route. I'll never forget the look on her face. The Jewish Community was celebrating in Battery Park. As we sat down to rest and enjoy the music, the band played "Country Roads" to the tune of "Hava Nagila". West Virginians are at home wherever they go. God, Bless you John Denver.

Chapter 15

Hostas, The Addams Family, & One Tacky Mess

IN MY NEIGHBORHOOD, we appreciate and respect individuality. None of the houses look the same nor are they in straight rows. The lots are bigger than normal. We are spread out but we know each other. We're all different but that's OK, too. It doesn't mean we don't privately judge each other. We will talk about you but we will always be nice to you.

You can tell a lot about people from how their house

is landscaped. At least I think I can. I have a degree in art and design. I'm always re-designing places in my head. I can't stop it. My house is one of the first houses you see as you enter the neighborhood. I feel that it puts additional responsibility on me to present a good first impression. Carolyn's house is across the street. It is the other first house at the entrance but somehow the responsibility was mine. That's not to say that her landscape and gardens aren't any good. Her flowers have a charm that is perfect for the style of the house. She has put so much mushroom compost (a polite way to market composted cow manure) into the flower beds that the plants wouldn't dare not look good. I can't see any way to change what she does. All her flowers are pink and purple. This tells you she is creative, loving, and imaginative. She also showed me the value of container gardening. Her pots are clay and in perfect descending size and order coming down the steps of her porch. She does the exact same thing every year and it looks perfect. Um. What does that tell you?

My yard is mostly taken up with flower beds. If I thought about widening a flower bed, Jim hurriedly dug up the grass because it meant less to cut. I've planted perennials. I've told people that I'm creating texture with different shades of green foliage. I'm giving the impression that my design is on a higher level. Actually, I've stuck with what grows well and makes me look good. If a plant fails to flourish, I get rid of it very quickly. People think I know what I'm doing. Hostas work great in my yard. They come back up every year and keep getting bigger. I have planted so many Hostas over the years, that Sandy calls my yard, "Hostaville, U.S.A.". She says she can feel the ground shaking when they all start to come up in the spring. My daughter says I'm going to be reported to Homeland Security for creating a "Hosta" environment. Until the intervention, I'm going to keep collecting them. I enjoy gardening but what this really says about me is that I'm a bit of a lazy gardener. I also use chemicals. I zap weeds, kill bugs, and spread fertilizer. My dad was one of the chemists who developed the "Sevin" insecticide so it's in my blood. I'm not a hippy and I forgot to turn my compost pile last year. Green can mean self-reliance, balance, and growth. I'll take it.

I have a neighbor that plants only yellow flowers. Their house is white with a yellow door and shutters. According to the Internet, this could mean intellect, optimism, and cheerfulness. It could also mean impatience, criticism, and cowardice. I need to get to know them better to be sure.

Libby never comes outside. Her parents gave her one bush each year, the first five years she lived in the house. They have never been trimmed and their descending heights look like the service bars on my phone. Once she sat out a pot of plants from a family funeral. She has never forgiven Lowes for both of her dogwoods turning out to be the same color. Not a nature lover.

Some yards are very symmetrical with an even number of bushes, all the same species, lined up in front of the house. Nothing changes. There is no color and no imagination. These are dull people.

Another neighbor tries every year to plant flowers in a garden area or pots. They always die. Bless her heart. She just doesn't have the green thumb but a good heart. I once told her that she needed to enrich her dirt. She just didn't get it.

There is always a house with nothing. I have re-designed that house in my mind many times. It's a blank canvas. They are minimalists.

One home has a small garden area near the front door where they plant some flowers each year. The rest is grass. It's good to know your limits, and do it well.

Tom planted tulips in a perfectly round flower bed in the center of the front yard. He carefully measured the distance between each bulb with a ruler. The first year the tulips bloomed, alternating red and yellow, in perfect spacing like soldiers. The next year, the bulbs naturalized doing their own thing. The whole flower bed quickly disappeared. Mother Nature lost that battle.

Number 113 seems to be a nice family. I did notice that every plant in their yard has thorns. They also wear a lot of black. I can't help wondering if they are related to the Adams Family. If they name a child Cleopatra, I'll know.

There are many houses with water fountains and little ponds. I have one that is so small, I refer to it as a puddle. These are happy people. There is one house that has the whole front yard taken up by an enormous pond feature. They have included every piece of yard art you can buy. There is a bridge and archway covered with plastic flowers. Tacky mess doesn't begin to describe this creation. I cringe every time I pass it. These people must be way more than happy. They must be hysterical.

I recently discovered a category I can use to label my gardening style, that might give it some class. It is "English Country Garden". I'll try it.

Chapter 16
Road Bumps, Bear, & Oreo Cookies

IF YOU LIVE in a neighborhood like mine, you must live with people's pets. Over the years, I've had five basset hounds and two cats. All of them were free which does relate to the saying that you get what you pay for, even though they were all pedigreed, sweet pups. They all shed and droll. The cats just showed up. One basset only left the yard to lick the grease off a neighbor's barbecue grill. You must have a good reason to walk that far. Another kept jumping outside the property line defined by an invisible fence. He then ran back and forth whining and barking because he was afraid to come back in. Then there was Big Mac who would lay next to the fence line listening to his collar beep its warning till the battery went dead, then just walked out of the yard. There is just nothing you can do if your dog is smarter than you are. Tad and Max liked to lay in the road and sleep. They were the official road bumps. A new neighbor stopped to come and tell me she thought our dogs were dead. The problem was, that they would lay side by side across both lanes. Carol drove up to Max in her Firebird which put her close to the ground. He was asleep and didn't move a muscle. She called his name and tapped the horn. He opened one eye. I couldn't film him and show Max moving any slower. He stretched and managed to get up on all four legs. He walked to the driver side door, looked over his shoulder at Carol, and barked at her. How dare she disturb him. Tad didn't move at all. Carol said, "Your dog has an attitude." Hambone had attention deficits and imaginary friends. When you took him out to do his business, he had to be reminded to focus and concentrate or you'd be wandering around the yard all day. He was intuitive and understood every word you said. I miss my buddy.

One family named all their dogs and cats "Dusty". This is brilliant if you have more than one pet. They all come when you call one name.

Bob had a dog named "Bear". He was a big, black, long haired dog. He loved children and would lay near them as they played outside. He would bark at them if they left the yard. Every mother appreciated the extra supervision. One summer day I looked out and saw Bear walking up my driveway with a whole loaf of bread swinging under his chin. He had opened the basement door and took the bread off the kitchen counter. I intercepted him and took the bread back. Bear was indignant. Bob got baby ducks for his children at Easter. Bear got into the garage and ate the ducks. He also ate the neighbors rabbit. Bob feeds Bear quality dog food. We think he must need more protein.

Bear liked to swim in the river to cool off. Every summer he would get so matted that Bob would take him to the groomers to have all the fur shaved off down to the white under coat. The first time this happened, I wasn't sure about the strange, skinny, white dog in our yard. My daughter said, "Mom, look at his eyes. It's Bear." His eyes?

Snoopy was mostly a German Shepard. He had one short ear that stood up and one long ear that flopped forward. He came down the street every day to say hello to my basset Max. They each came to the front door and barked. Max was too old to play but he appreciated the friendship.

Big Mac, another basset of mine, liked to walk over to the Raines Farm. They had Oreo cows, fainting goats, and a camel. The cows were white in the middle and black on each end. They were bred for a promotion of Oreo Cookies but the company decided not to use them. The goats didn't faint anymore. They had been desensitized by too many people trying to cause them to faint. The camel and Big Mac loved each other. Big Mac would come to the fence and whine. The camel would run over and lean its head down to put its nose next to big Mac's. We figured they each recognized another goofy looking animal. Jim said both animals looked like they were designed by a committee.

The Chihuahua down the street was the neighborhood bully. He roamed up and down the street looking for victims. Big Mac was asleep on the porch. Chi-bully came across the yard to bite him in the butt. If no one will take care of your dog when you go on vacation, there is a problem.

When Sandy was first married, her husband had a dog that didn't like anyone but him. This dog snarled at everyone. Her husband was the only person who this dog would allow near him or to touch him. While he was in the hospital for a ruptured appendix, Sandy had to push the dog's food bowl toward him with a broom. All he did was growl and snarl at her. He was ugly, too. This dog had no redeeming qualities. As she was trying to back the car out of the driveway, the dog tried to bite the tires and she ran over his nose. While at the vets she had him put to sleep. When her husband got home, no more dog.

Deana's Golden Retriever liked to cool off in Patty's goldfish pond. Every afternoon he would climb into the pond and sit and watch the fish. He never ate one.

Jackie was a Jack Russel Terrier. I called her the "Mighty Midget". She didn't like John's motor bike. He was riding it up and down the street. Every time he got to Jackie's yard, Jackie would run out and stand in front of John's bike stopping him. We had to go and tell her to leave him alone. Jackie was very proud that she could halt traffic. Merilee had a big party in the backyard while her mother was away for the weekend. Sandy knew something was up when she got home, because the house was spotless. She just didn't know what it was yet. As she sat outside on the patio, Jackie began bringing her beer bottle caps and dropping them at her feet. Sandy went over and lifted the garbage can lid. This Bud's for you! Jackie reveals all.

Mr. and Mrs. Hatfield had a very old toy poodle, that they adored. This poor dog was well past his due date. He was so fat and over fed that his legs were barely visible. He looked like a white fuzzy ball. Because he was blind, they had a system of baby gates to prevent him from falling down stairs or off the porch. During any visit, they explained the gates, many times, by stating, "that he is blind, you know." Conrad counted them repeating this information eighteen times during his visit. When their niece told Conrad that the dog had died, Conrad said, "I bet he didn't see that coming".

Mike is a big tough guy. He was a Navy Seal. You just can't picture him with a small dog. When he married Wendy she had two designer dogs that she loved equally. Mike loved Wendy. One was a Jack Russell/Shih Tzu mix. The other was an English Bulldog/Shih Tzu mix. They were adorable. I don't know what Wendy called them, but Mike called them, "Jack-Shit" and "Bull-Shit".

Chapter 17
Motorcycles, Hot Weddings, & Flying Cows

THE MORE YOU GET to know people and become involved in their lives, the more weddings you are invited too. I've never enjoyed going to weddings, but they can be entertaining when things go wrong   There are so many people and emotions involved, that the possibilities are good for entertainment value. Before my wedding, the editor of the local paper, wrote an editorial complaining about the long wait between the ceremony and reception while pictures are taken. I sent him a note with my invitation promising a 'no wait wedding". His follow up article stated 7.34 minutes from start to receiving line. He was first in line and particularly liked the choice of chocolate or vanilla cake. He ate a piece of both. We took pictures after receiving line duty and provided refreshments before cutting a separate cake for the bride and groom. A short wedding and a long marriage.

When Margo's only child, a daughter, was getting married, she determined that it would be the society event of the century. Thousands of invitations went out, all professionally addressed, using a special calligraphy style. A venue was rented to display the gifts, all of which were numbered, cataloged, and acknowledged. Margo re-gifted them for years. I know because I received several with the number tags still on them. Nancy was registered in all the leading Department Stores in the eastern United States. Limousines carried the wedding party from the cathedral to the reception at the country club. The wedding party later lined up to watch a helicopter take the bride and groom to the airport for a honeymoon in the Bahamas. Nancy was divorced within five years.

Kathy got married in a little country church that was destined to be torn down for a new interstate ramp. The photographer forgot to come. He was the groom's cousin. The marriage was finished before the ramp.

Roberts mother decided to get married at the last minute. No one could figure out why the hurry because she wasn't pregnant. The invitations were by phone and the theme was "covered dish". The ceremony took place in the living room of her double-wide trailer and the refreshments were located on the kitchen counter in Walmart deli containers. The last I heard, they moved the house to some family land in Kentucky.

Dawn's second marriage was located on new, river side property she and her husband to be had just purchased, up the river from our neighborhood. Dawn's daughter was in my Girl Scout Troop, with my daughter, so we were invited. Emily and I wore our best garden party dresses with matching dress sandals. The ceremony took place in a cinder block garage that was being turned into a small bar/store next to a mobile home called, "Grandpa's Pizza". A sheet of plywood, which served as the store sign, was placed on the pool table and covered with a blue bed sheet. One wall was covered with sheets of pastel bulletin board paper. Deli trays lined the bar filled with beanie weenies and a barrel was filled with ice cooling cans of beer and soft drinks. In the field behind the store a deer, out of season, was roasting on a spit. Five plastic chairs were in place for the grandparents. Everyone else stood. Music was provided by a cassette player and the bride wore a denim blue, floor length dress. The minister was in his late nineties with a long beard and a black top hat like Abraham Lincoln. He was someone's grandfather but no one seemed to know who. In his honor, they named the store after him and his was the fifth chair. I drove our Audi to the venue. The rest of the guests arrived on motorcycles wearing black and white skull design bandannas, tattoos, and chains. The best man wore hunting camouflage. He brought the deer. Emily and I were overdressed. As the ceremony ended, banjos, guitars, and kegs came out. Since Emily was still a minor we passed up the deer burgers and picked and grinned back home. I wave at Dawn every day when she delivers our mail. They just celebrated their twentieth anniversary.

I've seen a neon, plastic, cross, above the altar, blink on and off during the ceremony. One Father of the Bride tripped over her train and ripped it off the dress. One outdoor wedding unexpectedly took on a Celtic Theme when the maid of honor left the bridal party's shoes at home. They walked down the aisle in bare feet. One groom came out dressed like Darth Vader while the organist played his theme. At a beautiful candlelight, garden wedding, the bride's dress caught on fire. It was so voluminous that the groom and best man had to crawl under it to put out the fire. No one got hurt. There are brides and grooms who pass out during the ceremony. One dog/best man pooped in the center of the isle then lifted his leg on an usher.

Matt and his wife take the prize for the most things going wrong on a single wedding day. It was the hottest day of the year, so far, and rising. The humidity was in the ninety percentiles. As the groom was driving to the wedding, the top of his convertible flew off and he had to climb down the interstate embankment to retrieve it. The maid of honor's car broke down and she hitched a ride with two strange guys, in a pickup truck, who stopped to help. They delivered her safely to the church. The other bride's maid found that her shoes had melted in the trunk of her car. The zipper came out of the bride's sister in law's dress and she had to be sown into her dress. It was discovered that the ring bearer had grown out of his shoes. The mother of the groom, in full wedding dress, walked down the street to a Payless Store and bought shoes for her grandson and the bride's maid.

When I arrived, Cindy, the mother of the groom, had just returned from the shoe store and was mopping the sweat off her face and trying not to smear her makeup. She blurted out that her husband was searching the church for the ring bearer's pillow that has the rings tied to it. Luke could not remember where he left it. She asked me if I had more tissues because her boobs were sticking together. The air conditioning was struggling.

We left Cindy stuffing tissues in a hopeless lift and separate situation. We sat down with Cindy's sister as the mother of the bride arrived with a beehive hair style that Marge Simpson would envy. I heard her say, "My goodness she has her hair jacked up to Jesus!". She then asked if I had heard that the minister announced at the rehearsal dinner that he was gay. No, I missed that. The pillow was found. Luke laid it on a step, in front of the altar, put his head on it and fell asleep.

Sandy and I went to the reception alone. My husband Jim got called back to his office. There was an emergency at a well site. Sandy's husband Tony remained under their house installing a new sewer line.

The reception room was organized like a golf course. We were at the 17th hole/table with the newly gay minister who could not stop talking about it. He was talking like someone who just got religion. Sandy had just stopped using crutches after seriously breaking her leg and it was starting to ache. We propped it up on an empty chair and I went to get her food. I was told it wasn't the 17th hole's turn. I sat down to watch the candles singe the crust of a centerpiece which was made out of different types of bread. Sandy said, "I'm going to hurt him if he doesn't stop talking." I looked up at the top table and watched Cindy drink her forth glass of wine. Then the storm hit. It was later called a derecho. The water hitting the wall of glass panels, facing the river, was so heavy that you could not see out. The electricity went off. I swear a cow flew by. The disc jockey announced that he would lead us in a sing along. Sandy said, "I'm going to hurt him if he doesn't stop talking." Cindy was finishing glass six and leaning back on her chair. By this time, she couldn't care if it snowed oats. Jim texted that he was locked in the building till auxiliary power unlocked the security system. Sandy's husband was still trapped under the house, riding out the storm and sewage.

The rain stopped, and the sky turned orange. They announced that the wedding breakfast and picnic for the next day had been canceled. I got Sandy to the car. It took me four hours to travel fifteen miles to get us home. The last few miles we followed the Fire Department as they cleared trees from the road. The man on the radio announced that the area had just experienced a severe storm and asked us not to travel unless necessary. Sandy said, "I'm going to hurt him if he doesn't stop talking."

Chapter 18

Collecting, No Smoking, Motor Boat, Designer Rocks, Hoarding, & Wandering The Desert

I LOVE THAT WE REALLY LIVE in a small world. The more I study people, the more I see that we are all very much alike, and no one normal. I'm not sure there is a normal. Some of us cope better than others, in our own styles. In the South, different styles are celebrated. We call that character. People with a lot of "character" are called "Characters". I collect unusual names, antidotes, and "characters".

As a school librarian, I came across many unusual names. I struggled with my first homeroom class list. So many names were so closely similar, that could not keep them sorted out. Among the girls there was: Lashawna, Lashena, Latwana, Latesha, Lasheanna, Letasha, Latisha, and Latasha. Among the boys, there was: Lashawn, Leshawn, Lamar, Lemar, Treshawn, Jamel, Jamal, Jamile, Jamule, and Jemele. One child's middle name was Loverboy. Many children had names and middle names that were so original that the child didn't know how to spell all of them and the family was conflicted about how to pronounce them. There were some very unfortunate names, such as: Nosmoking pronounced nos-mo-king, or Shithead pronounced shi-teed, Pajama pronounced paw-ja-may, and Nosalir pronounce nos-a-lir which means no exit in Spanish. One year I had a complete bar. There was: Champagne, Tequila, Brandy, Chardonnay, Johnny Walker, Jack Daniels, Jameson, Gina, and Burgundy. We covered the globe with, Asia, Africa, America, Canada, and Europia. You know you're writing unusual names when spell check underlines most of the words in a paragraph. Depending on which version of Windows you are using, spell check wants to change my last name from Mottesheard to ministate, monistat, mottled, motherboard, or motor boat. The young lady playing the first chair, clarinet, in the school orchestra, was named, Claire Annette. The Band Director said he had no choice but to place her there.

One of my favorite characters was my friend Ellen. I miss her. For some reason, she reminded me of the British Actress Penelope Keith. I often called her Penelope. She watched the British comedy "The Good Neighbors" to see what I was talking about but never understood it. She was very detail oriented. She wore the same jewelry every day and explained repeatedly what each piece meant to her. She made sure you knew she was Jewish because in her words, she did not look Jewish. She had blond hair and blue eyes. She said someone got over the wall of the Ghetto. She often said funny things that only she could say. As a Christian Gentile, with brown hair, green eyes, and a German Heritage, I was only allowed to laugh.

She was a teacher who worked with children who were visually impaired or blind. Her records were impeccable and organized. Each year had its own color which corresponded to the color of paper she used that year and she kept a chart of the years and their color. A chart was created for every category of information. There was a chart of all the charts. She usually had five students, each in a different school throughout the county. Every day she kept track of each student's progress and provided specialized materials when needed. Because she had to travel from school to school she referred to herself as, "the wandering Jew". She said it was the perfect job for a Jewish Woman since it was part of her heritage to pack up and move from one place to another. The high school student she worked with had most of his classes in the wing of the school that did not have any water service. She said that her people were used to wondering in a desert. She called that part of the school, "Egypt". To this day, that part of the school is still referred to as either Egypt or the desert. They also, finally, hooked up the water fountains and bathrooms.

Soon after Ellen's mother died, she asked me where to find rocks that she could take to the gravesite. Since she would have to put them in her car, she didn't want dirty ones. I bought her some at local garden center. She was delighted with the perfect polished rocks I found. Whenever her supply was running low, she called me for more "designer" rocks.

Ellen was engaged to marry Tom in college. His family was Catholic and very wealthy. She wore her diamond ring, stayed close to Tom, but they never married because her father didn't completely approve. Tom didn't see a problem. Ellen could live any way she wanted. He owned five homes in different parts of the country, so she could also live anywhere. Tom offered to bring all her family and friends to The Greenbrier Resort for the wedding. Every time I felt like I needed a vacation, I tried to talk Ellen into getting married.

She dealt with Christmas by creating a character called Chanukah Claus. He wore blue instead of red. He came on the 26th of December and said, "Have I got a gift for you." This way he had time to take advantage of sales. I gave her a blue Claus every year that she put on a blue and white tree. She also collected Menorahs and ordered specially flavored unleavened bread for the holiday. She didn't feel that unleavened meant boring.

Ellen never made up her mind about the backsplash in her kitchen. She took a year to pick out a side table for the dining room, bought the same model and color car every four years, had her car detailed quarterly, felt that the Jewish custom of forgiving your sins for the year, in one day, more efficient than the Christian asking forgiveness and confessing all the time, she shopped for clothes every day, never let her gas tank fall below half, and collected stuffed animal lambs. You were a good, funny, thoughtful friend. I love and miss you.

Every day I encounter a character for my collection or something absurd that makes a good antidote. I collect candlesticks and sometimes have mild psychic feelings. Jim made me promise not to tell anyone. I bought the family sweatshirts, from an outlet store, after a trip to Florida. We wore them for three years before we realized that Florida was misspelled Floridia.

When Adam realized the misspelling he laughed so hard he got hiccups. At my local Bank, I often see Mr. Rogers who likes to hang out and talk. He dresses like a cowboy every day complete with Cowboy hat, boots, shirt, jeans, and two six shooters in a leather, hand tooled holster, that he made. He has never traveled outside of West Virginia. Nobody says anything to him about not bringing firearms into a Federal Building. Mrs. Johnson comes to the bank every day to check her balances and interest. She pulls a wagon with an elderly dog riding in it, right into the lobby. No one thinks this is odd. John rides his motorbike up and down our street whenever the weather is good. He almost has ten thousand miles on it. He wears a walkie-talkie and we consider him the neighborhood's mayor/homeland security chief. Kathy Mattea, the singer, is from a nearby town. At one time, her brother and sister-in-law Kathy lived near my neighborhood. Every time we had company from out of town, we would impress them by showing them Kathy Mattea's house. We just weren't specific.

Neva's father kept a shovel and cardboard box in the back of his truck. He picked up any roadkill he found. He said you just couldn't find good roadkill in the stores. He inspired a local roadkill dinner held every fall. He couldn't believe that Neva wasted good food to feed the squirrels in her yard for entertainment and not to be fattening them up to eat. Neva also kept a pair of gloves and a box in the trunk of her car. She saved turtles off the roads. By spring she had so many turtles that she gave one to each child in her Sunday school class. What a surprise for the parents on Easter Sunday.

I have to mention children as a source of laughter. My grandson is adorable, of course! Sometimes he is a pirate, a cat, a turtle, or a ninja. My daughter calls me every day with a funny story to share with friends. He is so much like his mother and uncle that I told my daughter it wasn't his fault. Lately, before he goes to the bathroom, he says either, "On your mark, go!" or "One, two, three, go!". I love it.

I celebrate what is odd, different, crazy, eccentric, loony, abnormal, a bit nutty, or absurd? I lost track of normal a long time ago. I'm not sure what that is and I'm certainly not qualified to determine it. I've found that people who appreciate and celebrate this part of life are much happier. I choose to be happy. You can't change, fix, or make this stuff up. That's why I collect and enjoy it. It is the best therapy. My advice would be to not try to figure it out. It might make your head hurt. I hope you have laughed with me.

About The Author

HEATHER is a native West Virginian. She grew up in South Charleston, the home of the "Black Eagles". When her husband built the house she designed, on the Poca River, she found that she and her future children would be living in the home of the "Poca Dots", the mascot of Poca High School. They originally were the Pocatalico Indians till she made posters, in high school, for a football game between South Charleston and Poca. They read, "ERASE THE DOTS" and "RUB OUT THE DOTS" designed to make fun of and humiliate the other team. Poca liked it however and changed mascots. Be careful, God has a sense of humor. Heather has not been able to adjust to that. This is where she and her friend Sandy became the "Hot Dog Queens" by selling 464 hotdogs in one football game.

Heather is a retired teacher and librarian, an artist, writer, and widow with two grown children and one grandson. She enjoys reading, gardening, history, interior design, and eating out with friends. Writing a book and having an ISBN or Library of Congress number is on her bucket list.

Made in the USA
Middletown, DE
06 December 2019